Tennessee River flatboat, early 19th century

Riverboat on Tennessee River (NARA)

*View across the Saulpaw Bridge in the late 1860s
(before it was destroyed by flood and replaced by the Gay Street Bridge
and before the Henley Street bridge was constructed)*

*USA Road Cycling Championship 2017,
Gay Street Bridge, by Bruce McCamish*

Created in 1933, TVA (Tennessee Valley Authority)
built the dams that made "the Great Lakes of the South"
as part of Roosevelt's New Deal

*Giant catfish, **Beneath** (2013)*

In a seemingly impossible feat, the author poses with his book,
"Lost Tales of Scruffy City," BEFORE it was published…

All profits from

"Lost Tales of Scruffy City Unauthorized Walking Tours"
will be donated to good causes like
Jack Neely's Knoxville History Project
and the Downtown District Association

Books by Scott West:

The Crook Books: Volume I
Lost Tales of Scruffy City: Volumes I-IV

Available at <u>ScruffyCity.Com</u>, TheCrookBooks.com
and at Earth to Old City, Preservation Pub and Scruffy City Hall
on Historic Market Square, Knoxville

A bit of the history of
Lost Tales Historic Walking Tour:

The first printing we did of Lost Tales was way back in the **1990s** when we self-printed a short walking tour, mostly gleaned from the historic gold-mining of local treasure **Jack Neely**. Back then we called it **Lost Tales of the Old City** and we were quite flattered when the words from our little sepia-toned brochure made their way to the cover of the *New York Times Travel Section*.

"'GUNSLINGERS, prostitutes, millionaires, derelicts, bootleggers, Confederates, bank robbers, train wrecks, weird science, mysterious deaths.' Not exactly the kind of description I expected to find in a welcome center brochure in Knoxville, Tenn. Printed on plain brown paper, the inauspicious pamphlet was almost hidden behind flashier counterparts touting the city's museums, restaurants and antebellum mansions."

--*New York Times* (**1999**)

We still are quite flattered but the scope of that scruffy little brochure has broadened…

Great Cities are Built on Great Crimes:
Lost Tales of Scruffy City
Unauthorized Walking Tour

The River Road

Also available:

The High Road

The Low Road

Highway to the Sun

Early map of downtown Knoxville

Preface

A quarter-century years later and some things never change. The best parts of this book are still based on the hard work and dry wit of Historian **Jack Neely**. Credit all interesting and properly researched stories to Jack. Direct all complaints for hearsay, rumor, gossip, plagiarism and pure speculative fiction to Scott West at **Market House Café** and **Earth to Old City** at 36 and 22 **Historic Market Square**.

Pick up copies of all Jack Neely's works, including: "*Knoxville's Secret History Volumes I and II*" and "*Market Square: The Most Democratic Place on Earth*" at great local businesses like **Union Avenue Books**.

If you read Jack Neely long enough, you'll get the feeling that Knoxville has figured in most of the events that make up this great nation's history.

Ghosts of cowboys and confederates walk the streets of **Scruffy City**. Legends like **Buffalo Bill, Kid Curry** and **Hank Williams** linger amid buildings listed on the National Register of Historic Places.

Knoxville's creative community thrives here in Knoxville's most authentic and vibrant collection of galleries, restaurants, shops and living spaces.

Evening entertainments, dinner dates, patio lunches with lovers of unique antiques, late lattes, nighttime strolls, afternoon desserts in all designs, inspired shopping, apparel buying, seeking the unique while accessorizing... **everything is art in Scruffy City.** For things to do (after you take our lovely walking tours), check out ScruffyCity.com and VisitKnoxville.org

Let's begin our pleasant *River Road Unauthorized Walking Tour* of Knoxville's great crimes— excuse me, grand and interesting past. We'll start across the street from the Andrew Johnson Building at 912 S. Gay Street. Mosey on south down Gay Street towards the historic bridge. Cross Gay Street at Hill Avenue and pause just before the Old Courthouse.

(Yep, this is the very same bridge that **Kid Curry** rode the sheriff's stolen horse across during his escape from the **Knoxville Jail** on his way to join **Butch Cassidy's Wild Bunch** in South America, and in the process helped jump start & extend **Knoxville's Prohibition**, wherein K-Town's ban on the sale of alcohol lasted 60 years, some 40 years longer than the rest of the country).

Amble one block east on Hill Avenue till you arrive at one of Scruffy City's most historic sites, Blount Mansion.

Blount Mansion

High Treason & Other Scandals with Our Founding Scruffy Scoundrels

Here on a street called Hill, a block east from the **Gay Street Bridge** and the **Old Courthouse**, you can visit an old homestead high above the Tennessee River, a place the **Cherokee** called "the House with Many Eyes," perhaps better known these days as **Blount Mansion**.

Knoxville's William Blount signed The Constitution with the other Founding Fathers (you know, Washington, Jefferson, Madison, Franklin...)

The Brothers Blount

William Blount (1749-1800), like so many movers and shakers in Scruffy City history, had his own share of troubles with the law (despite the fact that he wrote em, having signed **the United States Constitution** in **1796** with **Jefferson** and **Washington** and **Franklin** and the rest of his peers, you know, the **Founding Fathers**).

William Blount, Scruffy City scoundrel
and signer of the Constitution of the United States of America

Admittedly, Blount dozed through most of the meetings though, so perhaps it isn't surprising to learn that, in his boredom, it wasn't long before William Blount was impeached as a traitor for trying to get commissioned as a British officer, start a war with France and invade New Orleans. What?! Wait... Yes. But we're getting ahead of ourselves.

William Blount was a Scruffy Citizen long before there was even a Scruffy City from which to scandalize the new nation. Knoxville's original sinner had been around and involved in eyebrow-raising events long before any accusations of national treason, and he'd survived those just fine too, thank you very much. In one peculiar historical anecdote in **1780**, during a battle in the **Revolutionary War** for example, Blount lost the tidy sum of $300,000 in soldiers' pay…

During the **1783-84** sessions of the U.S. House of Representatives, it was William Blount who introduced the **"Land Grab Act"** (so named because it opened the lands west of the Appalachians to settlement). One individual who took advantage of this act was **Captain James White**, who acquired a tract of land that would later become Knoxville, Tennessee.

Another sly, sneaky bill introduced by Blount made soldiers with at least two years of military service eligible for land grants. Since most soldiers preferred cash to grants of land west of the Appalachians, many sold to Blount and other land speculators, some of whom were Blount's own brothers (helping explain how the **City of Brotherly Scruffiness** was born).

The French Broad River (circa 1900) merges with the Holston River to form the Tennessee River

In **1790**, **President George Washington** appointed William Blount governor of the new **Southwest Territory** (aka Tennessee). In **1791**, Blount chose **James White's Fort**, near the merging of the Holston and French Broad rivers, as his territory's new capital. He named the capital "Knoxville" after his superior, the United States **Secretary of War Henry Knox**, then gave appointments for governmental offices to friends like **John Sevier** and **Andrew Jackson**. It was also Blount who ordered a state constitutional convention be held at Knoxville in January **1796** after the **Lost State of Franklin** was more or less found and officially admitted into the Union as the state of Tennessee (from "**Tanasi**," a Cherokee word for meeting place). Whew!

*Map of the **Lost State of Franklin***

As the Governor of the Southwest Territory though (Tennessee's previous-previous incarnation), Blount negotiated the Treaty of the Holston in **1791**, bringing thousands of acres of Indian lands under U.S. control.

Chickamauga Cherokee Indian

Luckily for them, throughout the **1780s** and **1790s**, William Blount and his brothers had gradually acquired over 2.5 million acres in Tennessee and the trans-Appalachian west. Unluckily for them, however, in **1795**, the market for western real estate collapsed, and land prices plummeted.

Which brings us to the uncomfortable business of Blount and **high treason**... On the brink of bankruptcy, William Blount and Indian agent **John Chisholm** concocted a plan to conspire with Great

Britain to gain control of Florida and Louisiana, and in return, Blount was to become governor of the territory, receive additional large grants of land, and get free access to both New Orleans and the Mississippi River to boost the value of said properties.

However, when the conspiracy was uncovered in **1797** and turned over to **President John Adams** by Knoxvillian **Colonel David Henley**, Blount was expelled from the Senate, and gained infamy as the first federal official to face an impeachment trial. **George Washington** himself called for swift justice against Blount, and hoped he would be "held in detestation by all good men."

Rather than await trial however, Blount stole a horse and fled back to Tennessee, where he reckoned he'd be safe among other Scruffy City scoundrels.

Blount guessed right. Tennesseans didn't turn him over to the Feds. In fact, while a fugitive from justice in K-ville, Blount enjoyed a parade on arrival, and was re-elected to the state legislature in **1798**.

As for Blount's co-conspirator, Knox-villain **John Chisholm** remained in England in a debtors' prison for several months, then confessed the entire scheme to Congress upon his return, then disappeared from history. Other than conspiring with Blount to commit high treason against the U.S. of A., here is what little we know about this colorful character.

Born in Scotland around **1740**, John Chisholm was a large, lusty, hard-drinking, weather-beaten, pugnacious man with fiery red hair. He migrated to America in **1777** and lived among the Indians. Known to have married at least three times, Chisholm moved to **James White's Fort** with Governor William Blount in **1790**. It was he who built Knoxville's first tavern in **1792** (you guessed it, **Chisholm Tavern**) on the same block as the Blount Mansion, where he often wined and dined folks such as future President of the United States **Andrew Jackson** and Governor **John Sevier**.

Chisholm disappeared into the smoking-gun mists of history after Blount's impeachment though, leaving at least one wife and family in Knoxville to fend for their own frontiers without him. It is believed he disappeared into the Cherokee nation and went west with them in **1809**, presumably as lusty as ever.

Chisholm Tavern (Front and Gay),
photographed by the Historic American Buildings Survey in 1934

As for Chisholm Tavern, it stood at Front and Gay Streets, housing future presidents from **1792** through slum tenancies during the Great Depression till **1965** when it was demolished as part of Knoxville's now-notorious urban renewal.

Dr. John Mason Boyd monument at Knox County Courthouse

Belle Boyd Confederate Spy & The Boyd Sisters

Half a century after Blount's passing, Blount Mansion was inhabited by the **John Boyd** family during the Civil War. A trained surgeon, John joined the **Confederate Army** in **1861**. His mother and five sisters remained at Blount Mansion.

In **1863**, **Belle Boyd** (a cousin of the Knoxville Boyds) was sent from Virginia to Knoxville by **Stonewall Jackson** (for whom she had provided "much useful US Army intelligence," which is to say she was a **Confederate spy**). General Jackson sent Belle south to evade arrest by Federal authorities.

Portraits of Confederate generals Robert E. Lee and Thomas "Stonewall" Jackson.
(National Archives)

Belle's espionage career began when a Union soldier cursed at her mother. Whereupon, she pulled out a pistol and killed him. Although a board of inquiry exonerated her, Union sentries were posted around her family's house.

She then charmed one **Captain Daniel Keily**, and gathered "a great deal of important information." **Belle** conveyed her secrets to Confederate officers via her slave, **Eliza Hopewell**, who carried the messages in a hollowed-out watch case.

Belle Boyd, Confederate spy

Her spying didn't end there though. Belle hid in a parlor closet of the local hotel and eavesdropped on

Union General James Shields and his staff through a knothole she'd enlarged in the door. Later, in a sprint that left bullet holes in her skirt, Belle evaded capture to inform Jackson, "the Yankee force is very small... charge right down and you will catch them all." Which Jackson did.

Belle Boyd's notoriety preceded her to Blount Mansion. In her autobiography she tells of non-stop balls, parties, and riding excursions while sojourning in Knoxville. Ironically, in the fall of **1863**, (Belle's mortal enemies) the Union Army occupied Knoxville, and her refuge became known as the place where the seven ladies of Blount Mansion entertained Federal officers. Nineteen year old **Sue Boyd** would often play the piano and sing for them.

Sue was particularly fond of **General William P. Sanders**, a cavalry officer and bachelor. Their love story would end tragically though, after Sanders was mortally wounded in the **Siege of Knoxville** by a Confederate sharpshooter from the tower in a home known as **Bleak House** (under the command of his old roommate from West Point— more on that elsewhere).

Roll up Hill Ave. to the weeds of Blount Mansion Visitor Center on the corner of Hill and Gay.

Were Washington, Franklin and Jefferson…potheads?

After the lost tales of William Blount and the Boyd sisters, let's take a breather and look over the foggy **Tennessee River** below and the foothills of the **Great Smoky Mountains** in the distance, and consider the histories of both the breathing in & blowing out of hot air in America. And while contemplating those hazy trails, let's light into a brief hike into the wild weeds of historic hemp (aka Cannabis aka marijuana) in early America.

Washington & Jefferson, permanently stoned at Mount Rushmore

George Washington's Grow Log
and
Other Historic Hemp Hocum

Ben Franklin used hemp twine for his famous kite electricity experiment

In **1619**, America's first cannabis law was enacted in Jamestown Colony, Virginia. It ordered farmers to grow hemp.

By **1763**, farmers could be jailed for NOT growing hemp during times of shortage in Virginia. Hemp was legal tender. Farmers could pay their taxes with it in three colonies.

Not surprising, in addition to their original crime of high treason for conspiring to declare independence from the British in **1776**, Founding Fathers and other smugglers of note simultaneously conspired to capitalize on cannabis in its many forms.

Hemp farmer

A few old chestnuts for the doubters:

"Began to separate the male from female plants. . . Pulling up the male hemp. Was too late for the blossom hemp by three weeks or a month."
—**George Washington**'s Grow Log

Benjamin Franklin began the first commercial cannabis operation in America, by opening a paper mill using the fibers of hemp.

Our third president, **Thomas Jefferson** was in on the action too. He illegally smuggled potent hemp seeds from China into France, where hashish smoking was all the rage.

Not to be outdone, our fourth president and "Father of the Constitution," **James Madison** was heard to say that smoking hemp inspired him to found a new nation based on Democratic principles…

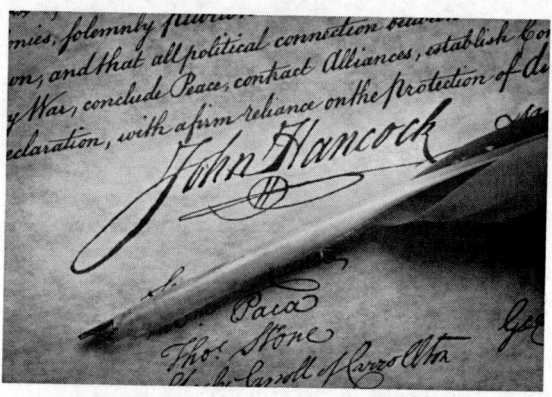

John Hancock's signature on the Declaration of Independence

None of this is surprising when you consider that until **1883**, around 90% of all paper in the world was made from cannabis hemp fiber. As follows, **Thomas**

Paine's "*Common Sense*," and the first two drafts of the *Declaration of Independence* were written on wacky paper. *The Gutenberg Bible*, the "Don't Tread on Me" flag, and **Lincoln**'s stovepipe hat were all woven from fibers of loco weed too.

Thomas Paine's "Common Sense" (1776)

By **1850**, the United States counted 8,327 hemp plantations (of over 2,000 acres) growing cannabis hemp for cloth, rope, canvas, cordage used for baling cotton, etc.

President Kennedy smoked weed for his severe lower back pain

Though **1937**'s cannabis prohibition law is still in effect in East Tennessee, nowadays marijuana is by far our #1 cash crop (2nd in the nation only to California). Much like the nighttime runs of bootleggers of the past in their souped-up 1926 Ford Model T Coupes and 1951 Ford pickups, smoke-running 1968 VW Vans and sleek cigarette boats are still making their moonlit runs across state and county lines today.

Stroll out from the Blount Mansion (east) side onto the walkway of Gay Street Bridge. Find a comfortable spot under the 13th streetlamp out on the bridge (for maximum awesome) and consider the Island Home shoreline in the near distance (well ok, imagine an island out past the giant Holston Gas tanks along the riverside)... Don't give a thought to the mole men infested limestone caves below the Tennessee River (we presume).

Gay Street Bridge by Jim Barnhart

Marble City Medusas, Mass Extinctions & Other Campfire Stories

Caves like this one in Kentucky were used as "stations" by "conductors" on the Underground Railroad, helping over 100,000 slaves escape to freedom by 1850

On the legendary **Underground Railroad**, "conductors" transported fugitive slaves at night and stopped at "stations" during the day to rest. These stations were located in hiding places like caves and hollowed-out riverbanks…

Prosperous Knoxville merchant **Perez Dickinson** was one such person rumored to have helped runaway blacks escape from southern slave-owners.

The limestone beneath the streets of downtown Knoxville is said to be honey-combed with caves. One such natural tunnel is even rumored to burrow to the far shore of the **Tennessee River**. Such ghostly whisperings suggest the possibility that these limestone corridors were once used as part of the Underground Railroad and as such might be haunted by the spectres of former slaves.

In the **1870s** (before the **Gay Street Bridge** was completed in **1898**), Island Home was a 600-acre farm criss-crossed by white picket fences owned by Mr. Perez Dickenson. (Oh yea, Perez was also first cousin of the famous poetess **Emily Dickinson**.)

Emily Dickinson

Mr. Dickinson's retreat still stands on what's now the campus of the **Tennessee School for the Deaf** (established in **1844** as the **Tennessee Asylum for the Deaf and Dumb**). Interestingly, Mr. Dickinson entertained guests at his riverside getaway, but never slept under its roof.

Island Home, Perez Dickinson residence

While we're on the subject of stone, before it was known as Scruffy City in the late 20th century, Knoxville was known by another moniker in the **19th**, "**Marble City**," due to its' quarries just south of the river, where beautiful stone was mined and traded worldwide.

Mead's Quarry (1893)

Marble City masons like those at **W.B. Fenton's Monumental Marble Works** (at **33 Market Square**) once busied themselves engraving gravestones for lynched criminals, decorated heroes and Union & Confederate veterans alike. You can see examples in **Old Gray** and the **First Presbyterian Church** cemeteries.

These days, just across the **Gay Street Bridge** in **SoKno** (south Knoxville), the value of those now-flooded quarries is that they provide amazing recreational opportunities for both locals and tourists alike in the 300+ acres of **Ijams Nature Center** and the 1,000+ acres of riverfront in **Knoxville's Urban Wilderness**.

Make sure to explore some of the miles of trails, climbing walls, swimming holes and waterways in the beautiful and idyllic spaces of lovely **Outdoor Knoxville**.

Exploring Ijams Nature Center

There is more than meets the eye in the wilds of south Knoxville. Under the peaceful surface of **Meads Quarry** at Ijams, blooms of freshwater jellyfish occasionally rise to the surface of the 25-acre lake like little sci-fi aliens.

These are the only species of freshwater jellyfish in the entire world, and in late summer when the water warms they come to the surface to reproduce in the ghostly umbrella-shapes we know best. Don't worry, they're only the size of a penny and harmless to humans.

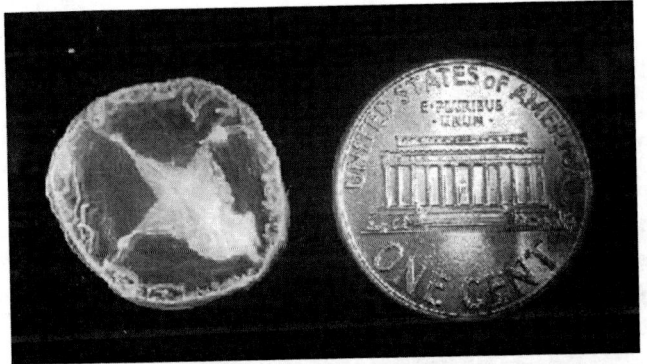

Freshwater jellyfish with penny for scale

The many-tentacled medusa-shapes of the jellyfish are to the life cycle of the medusa like the butterfly is to the caterpillar. Most of their lives are spent like transparent bowling pins waving their weird tentacles at the warm surface from 80' down at the cold quarry bottom.

But when the change comes, the jellyfish take flight to the edge of air and water, find one another in 300-armed embraces in the romantic last days of summer, and make sweet gelatinous love. As the season changes and cooler weather approaches, their eggs sink down to the muck… and all the Medusas die.

Kayaking Mead's Quarry at Ijams Nature Center (by Bruce McCamish)

By the way, jellyfish are good news for swimmers and canoeists alike. The tiny tentacled creatures are sensitive to pollution, so these near-invisible blooms are harbingers that the quarry water is clean and pure.

In addition to tiny jellyfish, East Tennessee is home to pygmy catfish (the size of the cap of a pen) too, as well as another famous minnow…

Snail darter and paperclip for scale

Tiny Fish
vs
Tennessee Valley Authority

A few miles west of here on the Little Tennessee River, in Lenoir City, a tiny two-inch fish halted construction of the **Tellico Dam**, at least for a while.

The **snail darter** is a species of fish discovered in **1973**, and listed as endangered under the U.S. Endangered Species Act of 1973.

In **1975**, legal controversy surrounding the snail darter lead to a U.S. Supreme Court ruling that halted completion of the dam, since it could make the snail darter go extinct.

In **1978**, however, a recovery plan to preserve the snail darter was hatched which involved transplanting the species into the **Hiwassee River** in southeastern Tennessee where it now happily darts upon its prey, snails (as you might have guessed) and insects in creeks and river bottoms.

P.S. The snail darter has indeed gone extinct from the Little Tennessee River since the completion of the Tellico Dam.

But for those who crave more than dime-sized jellies and pygmy felines, we have these too...

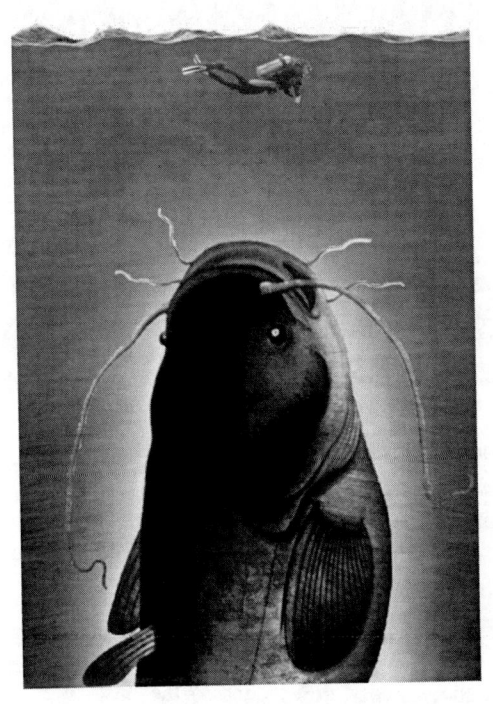

Giant Radioactive Catfish, Prehistoric Monsters & the Largest Salamanders on Earth

It may not just be in Tokyo that reptiles were made giant monsters by nuclear irradiation. Divers working at the bottom of TVA dams near Oak Ridge (where the radioactive fuel for atomic weapons was created) have reported Catzillas the size of school buses which could swallow a man whole.

Here's the fish story we've heard around the office water cooler: a diver swims down deep to the base of a dam to check for cracks, he sees a gigantic catfish that could swallow a VW whole in the murky depths of the lake, he frantically swims for the surface, but when he emerges his hair has turned white from the distress of his encounter, whereupon he vows to never dive again.

Artist's rendering of a mosasaurus having shark sashimi for brunch

Here in the wilds of South Knoxville, it's not just gigantic fish in the waters we have to contend with either. According to unexplained sightings and mysterious footprints, **Appalachian Bigfoots** and other hairy hominids lurk around the deep waterways and deeper forests.

Credence is given to these mysterious tales when one considers East Tennessee's distant past, back when prehistoric Knoxville was a shallow ocean.

Evidence of sea serpents exists in the fossilized bones of the zeuglodon (a wicked whale which grew to 70 feet in length during the Eocene Epoch 50 million years ago), and Mosasaur monsters (which prowled for prey during the Cretaceous period 70 million years ago). Both of these scary sea serpents disappeared (along with three-quarters of the plant and animal species on the planet) in global mass extinction events.

No worries. We're here because of those events, after all. Scientists estimate Earth has had about five of these mass extinction events (ice ages, super-volcano eruptions and cataclysmic asteroid impacts were the culprits).

As you may suspect, we're overdue for the sixth. Many scientists think it's already happening... and we are the cause. Our weapons of mass-destruction for this particular Armageddon are manmade climate change, massive habitat destruction and global pollution (Great Pacific Garbage Patch anyone?)...

And if those fail, we've always got a nuclear "winter is coming" backup plan for global annihilation .

Speaking of monstrous mutants, the **Great Smoky Mountains** are home to the biggest salamander in the world (the "hellacious" hellbender) and our neighborhood Jurassic Park has more biodiversity than just about anywhere else on Earth.

Allbright Grove virgin forest (Great Smoky Mountains N.P.)

Water and hydrocarbons exuded by the leaves produce the filmy "smoke" that gives these mountains their name. However, air pollution in recent years has added to the haze, cutting visibility back by 60 percent since the 1950s... and creating "acid rain."

Cosby Knob sunrise by Bruce McCamish
(Great Smoky Mountains National Park)

It was the leaders in good-ole coal-hazed Scruffy City that led the charge to create the Great Smoky Mountains National Park in order to preserve its grandeur for future generations. Called the "Father" of the Great Smoky Mountains National Park, **Colonel David Chapman** spearheaded the efforts to make a park in the Smokies, which by the **1920s** had suffered severely from industrial clear-cutting.

Lumberjacks pre-Great Smoky Mountains

*Black Bear inspects climate-change-causing automobile
in Great Smoky Mountains (1950s)*

Now, pretend you're a chicken and figure out how to get to the other side of the road...

Drawing of Knoxville in 1886 (before the Saulpaw bridge was replaced by the Gay Street bridge and before the Henley Street bridge was constructed)

However you arrive, you'll have a westward view from 80' above the water. You should be able to see Calhoun's Restaurant and Volunteer Landing below. Farther west, you should see the larger Henley Street Bridge and the University of Tennessee with its massive Neyland Stadium on the banks of the Tennessee River.

Streaking the Strip (Knoxville News Sentinel, 1974)

Streaking the Strip
through the
Underwear Capital of the World

Founded as **Blount College** in **1794,** the University of
Tennessee became U.T. as we now know it, in **1879.**

View from Henley Street Bridge overlooking the "Vol Navy' and Neyland Stadium by Bruce McCamish

"The Hill" at Blount College, established in 1794 (which became The University of Tennessee in 1879)

Cumberland Avenue is one of UT's most famous streets. The portion of that naked asphalt which streaks by the University of Tennessee is lovingly referred to as **The Strip**. The Strip got its nickname when **Walter Cronkite**, America's favorite national TV news anchor, referred to Knoxville as the "**Streaking Capital of the World**" after a mass-streaking incident in the **1970s**.

UT Chancellor Jack Reese and Police Chief Joe Fowler vowed not to tolerate any further displays of public indecency after a series of stunts on campus gained national attention, including fraternity-sponsored streak-offs, prize-giveaways at local bars and other outrageous acts of underclassmen.

UT's naturist exploits climaxed on the night of March 4, **1974** when the world got an eyeful of Scruffy City's best and brightest as 5,000 streaking students tooled down the street on everything from unicycles to fire trucks. The beer-fueled festivities even extended to the fiberglass bull mounted atop the popular hangout **Sam 'n Andy's**, the poor bovine barely surviving the night as dozens of simulated sex acts were performed on its horns and haunches. Luckily, cold and rain shrank the incident and its duration.

Knoxville was also once called the "**Underwear Capital of the World**" due to the prominent undergarment industry here.

Speaking of attention-grabbing undies, jockstrap-wearing, five-time MVP, Super Bowl Champion and the NFL's all-time touchdown leader, quarterback **Peyton Manning** played for the **University of Tennessee Volunteers** through his senior season in **1997**.

Of course, even our beloved Peyton isn't immune to a little Scruffy City controversy, especially in a chapter he's sharing with streaking underwear and illicit nudists. In **1996**, while still attending the University of Tennessee, Manning was accused of sexual harassment by a female trainer when he "accidentally" mooned her during a foot examination.

Kenny Chesney is another famous Knoxville entertainer known to bum around mostly in the buff at his paradise-home in the Caribbean. Chesney has sold 30 million albums (and change) and was the recipient of four consecutive Academy of Country Music "Entertainer of the Year" awards from **2005** to **2008**.

Knoxville native Kenny Chesney and Peyton Manning, pals ever since Peyton attended the University of Tennessee

Kenny Chesney and Peyton Manning have been best buds ever since UT's all-time passer played for the Vols. Then and occasionally afterwards, he and his pal Kenny Chesney have been spotted in **Uncorked** on **Market Square** and around downtown. (According to the staff, much like the rest of us, they tend to tip more with more drinks.)

In **2005,** Chesney married actress Renee Zellweger on the island of St. John, where he owns a mansion. After only four months of marriage, they announced their plans for an annulment. Zellweger raised some eyebrows when she cited "fraud" as her reason for ending their pseudo-marriage.

Renée Zellweger and Kenny Chesney on the island of St. John in 2005

Speaking of UT's preoccupation with human anatomy...

On the sometimes-foggy southern banks of the **Tennessee River**. UT faculty and students work late into the night studying decomposing body parts to help the **FBI** catch murderers and their ilk...

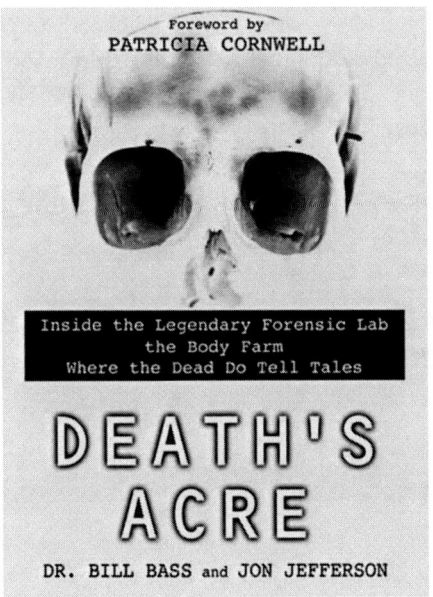

Dr. Bass and his bodies have more than a "passing" connection with Peyton and (four-time national-championship winner and Army brigadier general) Coach Robert Neyland.

On the other side of the Tennessee River from the Body Farm, UT's Forensic Anthropology labs are located under the football field in Neyland Stadium.

Like the 5,000 skeletons just dying to get out of Dr. Bass's closet, it's the largest such collection in the United States...

If you're digging the subject of famous bones, another University of Tennessee anthropologist, Dr. Richard Jantz theorized in **2018** that it was indeed **Amelia Earhart**'s skeletal remains that were found on an uninhabited atoll in the western Pacific. Soon after her stay at the Andrew Johnson Hotel in downtown Knoxville, the famous pilot (who had already been the first female to fly solo across the Atlantic Ocean in **1932**) was attempting to make a circumnavigational flight of the globe in **1937** when she disappeared without a trace after departing Papua New Guinea.

We would also be remiss in our discussion of forensics if we did not somewhere mention dark satirist **Kurt Vonnegut,** who studied mechanical engineering at the University of Tennessee as part of the Army Specialized Training Program before he was shipped off to **World War II** in Europe.

Captured in the **Battle of the Bulge (1944)**, Vonnegut was taken by boxcar to a **prison camp** south of **Dresden**. During his journey, the **Royal Air Force** bombed the prisoner trains, killing about 150 men. Thereafter, he lived in a slaughterhouse in Dresden, which the Allies furiously firebombed in February **1945**, killing 135,000.

Vonnegut survived by taking refuge with cadavers in a meat locker three floors underground. When he came back up, the entire beautiful city of Dresden was gone. The tale of those experiences was contained in his anti-war novel *Slaughterhouse-Five* (**1969**), which rocketed Vonnegut to fame.

Dresden, Germany after firebombing (1945)

Speaking of naturists, hippies, peaceniks and all things Knoxville, it should be noted that way back in the **19th Century**, K-Town had a bohemian youth culture long before Haight-Ashbury, the Left Bank or the Village.

Vagabondia Castle stone inscription, Volunteer Landing, the Hodgson's home from 1869-1872 (Dr. Katherine Leigh Carlson and her students, 2015)

In **1870**, just after burying her mother in **Old Gray Cemetery** on **Broadway** north of Downtown, **Frances Hodgson** returned to a dilapidated mansion at the end of **Walnut Avenue**. There, from her vantage overlooking the Tennessee River, she christened it **Vagabondia Castle**.

She then invited half a dozen relatives to live with her and follow their various muses in art and music, and attend lavish parties with her at **Lamar House** on **Gay Street** (now the **Bijou Theatre**).

Historic Market Square is where young Frances sold wild grapes to earn money for postage to mail her stories to publishers. Years later, **Frances Hodgson Burnett** published *Little Lord Fauntleroy* (**1886**), *A Little Princess* (**1905**) and *The Secret Garden* (which hasn't been out of print since it was published in **1911**). Two of the characters from *The Secret Garden* live on in a sculpture in Central Park's Conservatory Garden.

Elsie Leslie, America's first child star, as Little Lord Fauntleroy (1888)

Consider this: the big bridge west of you is called **Henley Street Bridge**. It's named after a man who stabbed an unmannerly but unarmed British prisoner when he was a 28-year-old **POW commandant** under **General George Washington** during the **American Revolution**. Although court-martial proceedings were held, Henley was acquitted and became Washington's "spymaster."

By **1793, Colonel David Henley** was Agent of the Department of War for the Southwest Territory under the original President W. It was here in law-avoiding Scruffy City that law-enforcer Henley sniffed out the treasonous plot of **Senator Blount** (yep, Blount Mansion Blount), basically while getting schnockered with a Blount co-conspirator in K-Town's first pub.

This is also the same Henley who gathered with a few other desperadoes on the creaky floorboards of Henley's old office on the corner of **Gay** and **Church** in **1796** for the purpose of creating their own state (also known as **Tennessee's Constitutional Convention).**

It was 29-year-old **Andrew Jackson** who suggested the Cherokee word "**Tanasi**" for the new state's name.

Look to the cliffs above and to the right of Gay Street Bridge as it scrambles onto dry land in SoKno.

In **1864**, during **the Civil War, Forts Stanley and Dickerson** stood on the high ground directly above the south end of what is now the Gay Street Bridge and were maintained by troops of the **1st U.S. (Colored) Heavy Artillery**.

Post-Civil War view University of Tennessee, Knoxville and Fort Sanders from Fort Dickerson across the Tennessee River

You can still visit Fort Dickerson, as it is now a city park just across the river.

Walk north, backtracking from the Gay Street Bridge and then take a left up the stairs by the Old Knox County Courthouse (1885). Investigate the monuments and statues there honoring famous Knoxvillians and events.

Knox County Courthouse, the "third" (1842–1886), which stood on Main across the street from the present courthouse

Bruce McCamish Photography

Downtown Knoxville and Tennessee River from Fort Dickerson Park

Moonlight paddle on the Tennessee River,
Henley Street Bridge in background

President George Washington and his cabinet: Henry Knox (Secretary of War),
Alexander Hamilton (Secretary of the Treasury),
Thomas Jefferson (Secretary of State) and Edmund Randolph (Attorney General)

Knoxville's namesake **Henry Knox** never visited
Knoxville. **Governor of the Southwest Territory** and
Superintendent of Indian Affairs for the Southern
District for the United States, **William Blount** named
the new capital after **Revolutionary War** general (and
George Washington sidekick) for the banal reason
that Knox was Blount's immediate superior.

(Inexplicably pertinent to this tour, Knox would later die in **1806** from an infection he contracted after swallowing a chicken bone.)

Knox County Courthouse cannons

Perhaps not in person, but in spirit, the **Secretary of War** does have a strong connection to Knoxville, as it was "hard" Henry Knox who formulated federal policy to expand west through the purchase of Native American land in treaties.

Monuments to Knox's success abound here on the Old Courthouse lawn, providing fascinating historical evidence in downtown Knoxville of America's dream of westward expansion, otherwise known as **Manifest Destiny**, "to establish on earth the moral dignity and salvation of man."

Federal Blockhouse erected by David Henley (1792), who commanded federal soldiers under General John Sevier to prevent Cherokee raids (art by Lloyd Branson), now site of the "Old" Courthouse

Getting that land— sorry, Manifest Destiny also meant sometimes expanding the territories of slavery along with the taking of Native American land. Of course, taking native land led to confrontations with native peoples (aka "**Indian Removal**") both in North America and later with islanders across the Pacific Ocean (aka "**imperialism**").

Treaty of the Holston monument on Knoxville waterfront

One of those Knox-formulated treaties is commemorated in a riverside monument on the east end of the parking lot for **Calhoun's on the River**. It was at **The Treaty of Holston (1791)** that **William Blount** negotiated the terms between the United States and the **Cherokee Nation**, under which the Cherokee came under the "protection" of the United States, with the United States managing all future foreign affairs for all the Cherokee tribes. Nothing to feel guilty or judgmental about... all completely legal...

"The Hiker" by Theo Alice Ruggles Kitson, Old Knox County Courthouse

Up here at the Old Courthouse, **Kitson**'s *The Hiker* **(1940)** memorializes in bronze the American soldiers who fought in the **Spanish-American War, the Philippine-American War and the Boxer Rebellion** (all three conflicts were for Manifest Destiny territorial expansion by the United States at the turn of the 20th Century). "Hiker" was a term soldiers of the period used to describe themselves.

Also here is an arched marble monument to diehard Confederate **Dr. John Mason Boyd** (of the Blount

Mansion Boyds) which faces the Gay Street/Main Street intersection. Then there's a monument to Knoxville's status as the first capital of Tennessee.

Finally, perhaps in homage to Andrew Jackson's many mental duels with Knoxville's John Sevier and their eruption into physical violence, here is the gravesite and obelisk memorial of Tennessee's first governor (and famous Indian fighter), **John Sevier**.

Memorial to John Sevier, Tennessee's first Governor

A huge crowd gathers for the second funeral of John Sevier. His remains were exhumed from the original grave in Alabama and interred next to the Knox County Courthouse (photo courtesy of the Tennessee State Library and Archives)

Don't mourn the lack of an Andrew Jackson monument here however, since citizens of Knoxville and every other town in the country exchange tiny $20 monuments to Jackson every day, including here on the grass over Sevier's grave. (Of course, Andrew Jackson despised banks, so he might be rolling over in his.)

Linger amongst the monuments and statues at the Old Courthouse. When you're ready, lean against a cannon, stand by a rifle or sit on a step and read on.

Knox County Courthouse (1903)

As a circuit-riding judge, holding court in Nashville, Jonesborough, and Knoxville (which was then the state capital), **Andrew Jackson** was here quite often back in the **1790s**, so often in fact that he kept a room in K-Town. Although the exact location is unknown, it was probably somewhere around the streets of **Church** and Gay (where we now enjoy many choices in surface parking).

Engraving of European gifting Native American alcohol

A Tale of Two Trees: An Old Hickory and a Sequoyah

"Red Eagle," surrenders to Andrew Jackson at the end of the Creek Indian War (Library of Congress)

Scots-Irishman **Andrew Jackson** was born in **the Carolinas** in **1767**. As a boy growing up in the rowdy **1770s**, he listened to countless stories of Indian "savages" and their heathen violence toward European settlers. At about the same time, a **Cherokee** boy named **Sequoyah** was born in an Overhill town called **Tuskeegee** near **Fort Loudon** along the **Tennessee River** (about an hour's drive from here). Both boys grew up without ever meeting their father.

As a child, Jackson served as a courier for the local militia during the **Revolutionary War**, during which he was captured by the British in **1781**. During his captivity, he was slashed and scarred on his forehead for refusing to clean an officer's boots, then starved and held captive with a near-fatal case of smallpox. He survived. Two of his brothers were less fortunate though and died at the hands of the British. Andrew's mother then perished from cholera while nursing prisoners-of-war on ships in Charleston Harbor, leaving young Andrew orphaned with only intense anger as kith and kin.

Young Jackson refusing to clean Major Coffin's boots during his childhood Revolutionary War service (1876 lithograph)

Like Andrew, Sequoyah was injured during his youth, his foot maimed in a hunting accident, leaving him with a limp for the rest of his life. The young Cherokee took over his mother's trading post after she passed away, where he began overindulging in whiskey. Sequoyah's trading post became a meeting place for Cherokee men, where he spent much of his time drunk, till the day he turned away from firewater for good.

Meanwhile, toward the end of the 18th century, Jackson was elected Tennessee's first representative to Congress.

While serving his young country, the firewater-tempered Jackson perceived endless sleights to his honor from peers, and challenged various men to duels to the death. Historians guess between 10 and 100... In fact, Jackson is the only U.S. President to have ever killed a man in a duel. He was also the first U.S. President to experience an assassination attempt (which was foiled by **Davy Crockett**).

Jackson even challenged Knoxville's **John Sevier** to a duel in **1803**. As the story goes, Jackson and Sevier saw each other right across the street from here and began arguing. Jackson accused Sevier of bribery and fraud, claiming Sevier had changed the original land claims for the state of Tennessee. In return, an incensed Sevier accused Jackson of adultery (and since Jackson had married his wife while she was still married to another man, technically both men were pretty accurate.) These accusations led to shots being fired between the governor of Tennessee and the state supreme court judge.

Although neither was hurt, the next day Jackson sent Sevier a letter challenging him to a duel. Since dueling in Tennessee was illegal, the men and their seconds set off for Virginia to settle the feud. However, en route the judge and the governor began exchanging insults. During the heated argument, Sevier's horse ran off with his firearms, whereupon Jackson pulled out his own pistol and began chasing Sevier, who had to hide behind a tree while Jackson calmed down.

Andrew Jackson vs Charles Dickinson duel

In **1806**, during yet another duel, Jackson wound up with two broken ribs and a bullet lodged in his lung. After the order to fire was given, his opponent **Charles Dickinson** (credited with 26 previous dueling kills) turned and shot Jackson in the chest, missing his heart by two inches.

According to witnesses at the event, Andrew Jackson just stood there as if Dickinson had missed. Jackson then took careful aim and delivered a fatal bullet to Dickinson's gut. As for Jackson, the bullet he carried from Dickinson's shot caused him to frequently cough up blood throughout the rest of his life.

Andrew Jackson bust in Metropolitan Museum of Art by Hiram Powers (1839)

Jackson's injuries from brawls and duels didn't calm his mercurial temperament, however. He resigned from Congress and became major general of the Tennessee militia under **Governor William Blount** of Knoxville, where we presume he could better express his proclivities toward violence. Governor Blount authorized Jackson to mobilize troops for a southern expedition against Jackson's favorite enemies, Indians and Brits.

The branches of the two Tennessee trees intersected at this point. Sequoyah enlisted on the side of the United States under General Jackson to fight **British redcoats** and **Creek Indians** in the **War of 1812**.

In this period, Jackson earned the nickname "Old Hickory" from the soldiers under his command (because he was tough as old hickory wood).

Meanwhile, Sequoyah noted that he and the other Cherokees were not able to write letters home, read military orders, or record events like the white soldiers.

While other Cherokees thought this paper transmission of information a form of sorcery, Sequoyah resolved that he would one day create a writing system for his people.

In **1814**, Jackson became a national celebrity when he crushed a tribe called the **Red Sticks** at **Horseshoe Bend**, ending the Creek War. However, his troops might have been repulsed had the Cherokees not crossed the river and attacked the Creeks from the rear.

A Cherokee named **Junaluska** saved Jackson from an attacker that day, prompting the future President of the United States to declare, "As long as the sun shines and the grass grows, there shall be friendship between us." (Sadly, in the peace treaty he negotiated with the Creeks, Jackson confiscated 23 million acres of Indian land in Alabama and Georgia.)

Complicating our modern view of Jackson and Native Americans, after the slaughter of a Creek Village, Jackson adopted an orphaned Indian child named **Lyncoya**.

Also, when Jackson arrived in **New Orleans** and imposed martial law in December of **1814** contingents of free black soldiers and loyalist Creek Indians joined him. (It probably didn't hurt his camaraderie with his troops that Jackson smoked marijuana with them.)

Promoted to major general in the U.S. Army in **1815**, General Jackson defeated British forces at the **Battle of New Orleans**, making him a national hero of the "Second American Revolution."

Meanwhile, Sequoyah returned home and worked for over a decade to perfect his invention of the Cherokee written language. Even after his own wife burned his work, believing it to be witchcraft, he persisted. In **1821**, Sequoyah succeeded in distilling Cherokee oral traditions into an alphabet of 86 symbols. The Cherokee officially adopted Sequoyah's written language and used it to write a constitution.

Sequoyah statue by Daniel HorseChief (2010)

By **1825**, even as white squatters flooded onto their native lands, the Cherokee tribe enjoyed a higher rate of literacy than the trespassers on their lands who called them savages.

One by one the other major southern tribes—the Chickasaws, the Choctaws, the Creeks and the Seminoles—signed treaties that required them to be removed to the far side of the **Mississippi River.** During the early **1830s**, over 120,000 Native Americans who lived on millions of acres of land in Georgia, Tennessee, Alabama, North Carolina, and Florida were forcefully removed from their ancient homeland.

But still the Cherokees held out…

At last, in **1838**, worn down and overwhelmed, 16,000 Cherokees were corralled by US troops into holding camps to await removal to Oklahoma under **President Andrew Jackson's Indian Removal Act.**

Indians who tried to flee were shot, while those who waited in the camps died from malnutrition, dysentery and assaults by the troops who guarded them. Under orders from the man who'd been saved by one and had adopted another, the Cherokee were marched 800 miles to Oklahoma during a bitter winter, known by its survivors as the **Trail of Tears**. One-fourth of the Cherokees died during the relocation.

Davy Crockett was the only Tennessee Congressman to vote against the **Indian Removal Act**, and this unpopular decision cost the legendary bear-hunter his seat, even though he had fought with General Andrew Jackson in the Creek War and had later wrestled President Jackson's would-be assassin to the ground.

After losing reelection in **1835**, Crocket told his fellow East Tennesseans, "You may all go to hell, and I will go to Texas."

Three months after arriving there though, the adventurer who claimed to have killed a bear in total darkness by plunging a knife into its heart, died with 200 other men fighting for the Republic of Texas at **the Alamo** Mission in San Antonio against the army of Mexican **General Santa Anna**.

Davy Crockett's last stand at the Alamo

Interesting side note: Davy Crocket boasted in **1825** that he'd killed 105 bears in seven months in the backwoods of East Tennessee.

Knowing that, now consider this: 150 was the entire population of black bears in what would become the **Great Smoky Mountains National Park (1934)**.

*Davy Crockett claimed to have killed 105 bears in 7 months
in 1825 in the backwoods of East Tennessee*

Davy Crockett campaigning for Tennessee Congress outside a saloon

Sequoyah on the $20 bill, it just makes sense

Sequoyah also perished in Mexico, not in battle but while searching for lost bands of his people and working to reunite the Cherokee Nation. His written language lived on, however. His Cherokee alphabet was carried around the world and used to create over 65 other languages for groups in places as far away as Africa and China.

Needless to say, countless American landmarks are named after Andrew Jackson (including, we presume, Jackson Avenue on this very walking tour).

Perhaps a tad more surprising, Sequoyah's name lives on in Scruffy City too.

Sequoyah Hills was one of Knoxville's first suburbs, and today is home to some of the city's most affluent residents. Curving through Sequoyah Hills like the Tennessee River beside it, **Cherokee Boulevard** is home to Knoxville's first **Dogwood Arts Trail**, established in **1955**.

The **Tennessee Valley Authority Sequoyah Nuclear Plant** bears his name also. Perhaps more fittingly, where the legendary **Appalachian Trail** crosses its summit, **Mount Sequoyah** has an elevation of 6,003 feet above sea level in one of the highest and most remote places in the **Great Smoky Mountains**.

Appalachian Trail in Great Smoky Mountains
by Barry Hill

Exit the Old Courthouse grounds between the cannons and go down the stone steps to Main Street. Walk left to the red brick crosswalk that will soon carry you like Dorothy and Toto across K-Town's Main Street to the Land of Oz otherwise known as the Federal Courthouse.

We must turn our gaze away from the powerful neutrality of the federal government for a moment and face the more immediate righteous impartiality of local judgement awaiting us in the City County Building at 400 Main Street.

The face of the City County Building looms above the **Tennessee River**. But… I tend to think of this as the rear entry.

The City-County Building was completed in **1979**, thanks to the efforts of legendary local businessman, football star and founder of Pilot Oil, **Big Jim Haslam**.

Perhaps it goes without saying that it houses the offices of both city and county governments, but it also houses the **Knox County Jail** and all those denizens of the drunk tank. Literally, ten stories tall and bullet-proof, at the time it was built the Knoxville City County Building was the largest office building in Tennessee.

Nonetheless, immediately after opening, the jail struggled with overcrowding. In **1986**, a class action lawsuit was filed in federal court, claiming the jail was too crowded, and three years later, a judge ruled the facility unconstitutional. When the county failed to resolve the issue, the judge ruled the county in contempt of court, forcing the county to build a new facility, which opened in **1994**.

While on the subject of jails, we are obligated to tell the story of **Lonas Ray Caughorn**. Born in **1926**, Lonas Ray became a leader of the safe-cracking "Tennessee Torch Gang."

In **1958**, Caughorn escaped from the State Prison in Nashville, TN, and was later captured in Atlanta, GA, accompanied by a red-haired, Knoxville girl named Kathryn Louise Underwood, whom Lonas Ray had married several days earlier... and divorced several days later...

The "Hoosgow Houdini" vanished from the **Knox County Jail** on May 6, **1959** as one of many such prison performances. And, much like **Kid Curry** before him, Lonas Ray escaped K-Town justice. For his many jailbreaks and endless criminal derring-do, in **1960**, Lonas Ray was sent to inescapable **Alcatraz** in San Francisco. Alcatraz was designed to hold prisoners who continuously caused trouble at other federal prisons.

Two years after he was released from yet another prison in **1969,** Caughorn was killed by a farmer and his son during a robbery attempt in Louisiana. He is buried in **Woodlawn Cemetery** in Scruffy City.

One colorful native who worked in the City County Building from **2010-2018** was Knox County Mayor **Tim Burchett** (born in **1964**), who, while serving in the **Tennessee State Senate (1999-2010)** gained fame for sponsoring the "**Road Kill Bill**." The Road Kill Bill made it legal to take coons, rabbits and possums (who met their untimely ends under not-such-a-Goodyear tires) home for stews, casseroles, kabobs and fun fricassees for the whole family.

That's the thing about possum innards:
They's just as good the second day!

Buddy Epson in The Beverly Hillbillies, an American sitcom from 1962 to 1971.
The Clampetts are a poor backwoods family who move to posh Beverly Hills,
California, and are the stereotype of East Tennesseans to many non-southerners

Needless to say, the Road Kill Bill spawned a million Tennessee-hillbilly jokes around the world. In one of his **Tonight Show** monologues, **Jay Leno** suggested Tennessee's state motto should be changed to "Fender-Lickin Good."

Bumper stickers like "Possum— the other white meat" popped up around the state like a mole invasion, even as an officer of the **Tennessee Wildlife Resources Agency** declared that "no wildlife officer would have charged a citizen with possession of road kill with intent to eat" (even if he did).

As if pre-cognizant of this very walking tour, Mayor Burchett declared November 16, 2012, "Official Knox County Bigfoot Day."

While we're on the subject of cryptid hominids in and around Scruffy City, we would be remiss if we did not delve deeper into the subject most keen to Mayor Burchett's heart, the **Bigfoot of the Appalachians**.

On **February 24, 2013**, **Animal Planet** filmed Season 7 Episode 1 of *Finding Bigfoot* ("Peek-A-Boo Bigfoot" remains one of the highest rated episodes of the series).

On any given day, you can most likely meet one of the Bigfoot Hunters from that episode on **Historic Market Square** (he's the one in the Mayberry overalls and the Schlitz Malt Liquor ball cap).

With a team of professional hog callers, a national TV film crew and Animal Planet in tow, troubadour **Andy Pirkle** (of the infamously womanizing band The Barstool Romeos) hunted the elusive **Sasquatch of the Great Smoky Mountains** in the dark of night.

We'll let Pirkle himself tell you if they were successful in their hairy quest. Admittedly, Mr. Pirkle consumed quite a bit of **Cocke County moonshine** whilst on the hunt that night and is a bit fuzzy on some of the details.

PIRKLE SQUATCH

Tim Burchett's seat in the Tennessee Senate was taken by an even more colorful local politician, **Stacey Campfield** was first elected in **2004** to the Tennessee House of Representatives.

In **2005**, Campfield (who is very very white) said that he was interested in joining the legislative **Black Caucus**.

In **2011**, he proposed the "**Don't Say Gay**" bill to ban teachers from teaching about homosexuality in Tennessee's public elementary and middle schools.

Also, while serving East Tennessee, Campfield put forward a bill to tax the sale of pornography, sex toys, strip clubs and escort services in the state and use the money to remove the sales tax on groceries (the "Tax Porn Not Corn" bill).

In a **2012** interview, Campfield replied to a question on the history of AIDS, "most people realize that AIDS came from the homosexual community – it was one guy screwing a monkey, if I recall correctly, and then having sex with men. It was an airline pilot, if I recall…"

*Representative Campfield shocked the monkey (and other primates)
during his discussion on the origins of the AIDs epidemic*

In **2012**, Campfield was asked to leave the Bistro at the Bijou on **Gay Street** (fittingly) by owner Martha Boggs, who explained "I think he needs to know what it feels like to be discriminated against."

Politicians like Campfield inspired local comedian **Trae Crowder "The Liberal Redneck"** to go on a rant on YouTube in **2016** about the debate concerning trans-gender persons and their use of public restrooms. After his Liberal Redneck videos went viral, Crowder began a stint as the official "Hillbilly-in-Chief" for the **New York Daily News**.

Trae Crowder "The Liberal Redneck"

Crowder went on the road in **2017** with fellow comedians **Drew Morgan** and **Corey Ryan Forrester**. Together, the Ménage à Trois of Redneck Comedy authored *The Liberal Redneck Manifesto: Draggin' Dixie Outta the Dark* (**2016**) and rolled out to L.A. to film Crowder's FOX TV sitcom (we assume in an over-stuffed 1921 Oldsmobile Roadster just like the Beverly Hillbillies).

*The Liberal Redneck Manifesto, get a copy
and get some laughs with yer learnin*

Take the red brick crosswalk across Main Street and through the gates into the courtyard of the Federal Courthouse. Stop on the cobblestones in the middle of the expansive judicial complex which occupies the entire city block.

Gay Street Bridge, Plaza Tower and downtown Knoxville from the south bank of the Tennessee River (by Bruce McCamish)

As surveillance cameras look at you, look east across the statues of blind **Justice** and through the trees above the **Federal Courthouse** rooftop, where you can see the top of Knoxville's tallest building, the **Plaza Tower**. Note the sky reflecting in the mirror-windows. Now, reflect on this...

A century after **Joseph Mabry** (the man who gifted Market Square to the city of Knoxville) became a general in the **Confederate Army** and died with his son in a shootout, another tale of criminal bankers and family tragedy occurred on Gay Street, involving brothers **Jake and C.H. Butcher**.

1982 World's Fair postcard

Despite derisory projections of national voices like **The Wall Street Journal** (which wrote "What if they held a World's Fair and nobody came?"), as well as local power-brokers like **Cas Walker** (who denounced the idea as a "boondoggle"), **the Butcher Brothers** stood with **President Ronald Reagan** and celebrated the success of **the 1982 World's Fair**, for which they were known as the primary promoters.

Lamer Alexander (left) Ronald Reagan and Jake Butcher at the opening of the 1982 Worlds Fair

Their **United American Bank** was responsible for over 50% of Knoxville's business loans at the time, and was headquartered in their freshly finished 27-story Plaza Tower at 800 South Gay Street. Though built by UAB in the **1970s**, the Plaza and her sister **Riverview Tower** are still Scruffy City's tallest buildings.

The story didn't have quite as celebratory an ending for Jake and C.H. Butcher as it did for their World's Fair, however...

On November 1, **1982**, 180 federal bank regulators raided the their 29 banking branches and offices, where they discovered evidence of illegal loans, forged documents and various other forms of fraud, precipitating the fourth largest bank failure in U.S. history, and sending Jake and C.H. each to a 20-year prison term. It was rumored that some of that banking fraud went towards creating Scruffy City's successful World's Fair.

In our *Lost Tales Unauthorized Walking Tours,* we've talked about the war-torn **Boyd Sisters** in the **19th century**; we've delved into the bank-defrauding world of the **Butcher Brothers** in the **20th**; we've enlightened ourselves on the **Mabrys** and their three generations of slave-holding, war-profiteering and death-by-gunfighting in downtown Knoxville's streets...

Now we turn to the more peaceful tale of the **Wild West Brothers** here in the East and their conspiracy to distribute marijuana and launder millions of profits into preserving and rebuilding historic addresses on Market Square, for which their serial victim (the United States government) sued for justice... and won.

Market Square Drug Co. at Wall Avenue (circa 1909)

Twenty-four years after the Butcher Brothers may have committed fraud to bring the world to Knoxville, two other brothers responsible for helping tip the scales of **21st Century** revitalization, were themselves found guilty of another creative but illegal financing scheme on behalf of downtown Scruffy City (**2006**).

The West Brothers invested millions of marijuana profits into six condemnable addresses along the east side of Market Square in a successful effort to help revitalize the city center.

18-22 Market Square, building inspector looks at collapsed roof at WesTrent Lofts, what would soon become the roof of Uncorked (circa 2000)

Mike and Scott were sentenced to 105 and 75 months in prison, respectively, for their conspiracy. (While we're on the subject of crimes that will not be crimes in a few years, consider this morsel: it is also against the law to lasso a fish in Knoxville.)

(In an interesting anecdotal connection between the Wests and Butchers, the city of Knoxville discussed the Wests as prospective operators of the Sunsphere on World's Fair Park in 2006.)

We know Knoxville is on the right track regarding outdated laws however, as illustrated in **2018**, when **Mayor Madeline Rogero** was asked to look into the legality of the notorious Wests having rooftop bars at **Preservation Pub** and **Scruffy City Hall** on Historic Market Square. Her Director of Public Relations responded that he knew of no laws against rooftop bars, but thought Knoxville still had "a law against drinking and dancing."

Mayor Rogero, known to enjoy both of those activities (and in public) said, "Wait, we have what?" Yes indeed.

One assumes the City Council of **1962** was very concerned with discouraging certain behaviors of which dancing reminded them, and so our forefathers enacted a simple law: "No drinking beer & dancing allowed in Knoxville."

"The City with More Balls Than Most" realized the outdated ordinance kind of made Knoxville sound like the town in *Footloose*, so the wise souls of our City Council quickly removed the rather joyless legislation of yesteryear.

*A chapter from **The Crook Books Vol. I: Good-Intentioned Bad Guys**, which tells the story of the Author's light-hearted romp through the Federal justice system (2017)*

Exit the Federal Courthouse on the opposite side of the plaza from which you entered. Once outside the wrought-iron gates (West Entrance), find a comfortable spot, and read on.

Note the many law offices inhabiting the grand historic buildings along **Market Street**, once known as **Prince Street**. All river-ferried goods once flowed uphill to the bustling Market House, at least till the railroad arrived a few blocks north of town, ending the river commerce era.

Legal counselors in these buildings have represented gunslingers and politicians, bankers and priests, Butchers and Wild Wests, butt-chuggers and football players, good-intentioned lawbreakers and bad-intentioned criminals.... Be thankful you're not in need of their services… yet.

Wait. **Butt-chuggers**!!!???

Well, yes. The Pi Kappa Alpha fraternity chapter at the University of Tennessee was indefinitely suspended in **2012** following an incident in which a student was dropped off at **UT Medical Center** at 1:30am with a blood alcohol level of .45 (legally intoxicated in Tennessee is .09). Authorities believed the Pi Kappa Alpha member had used an alcohol enema (translation: he'd "butt-chugged" wine).

Steve Harvey discussion on the dangers of butt-chugging

As expected, in what some called the press conference of the century, it was exposed that the student had been specifically butt-chugging Franzia boxed wine in a "Tour de Franzia" of his bottom. The **UT Vice Chancellor for Student Life** called the incident a "black eye" for the university.

Six years prior, the bar was set for this nationally-televised misdemeanor by another famous Knoxvillian (and a favorite guest on our walking tours), **Johnny Knoxville**. Mr. Knoxville gained fame with his **MTV-**series of stunts, pranks and skits called *Jackass* in **2000** and a **2002** film compilation by the same name. Following those successes, he released *Jackass Number Two* in **2006**. This unusual box office hit contained a scene in which fraternities like Pi Kappa Alpha might have been introduced to butt-chugging.

*Knoxville band **King Super and the Excellents** model clothing referencing an unusual practice in Knoxville history*

Well, alrighty then…

Cross Cumberland Avenue and walk northward along the sidewalk of Market Street for two blocks toward Market Square, passing W. Church and Clinch Avenue. On your right, you'll see a menagerie of sculptures amid Krutch Park's intimate waterways.

Tennessee Williams with Knoxville aunt Ella Williams in a 1957 Knoxville News Sentinel photo

Being within a stone's throw of Gay Street in a garden of art is as good a time as any to broach another subject locked in a lover's embrace with Knoxville history.

In **1957**, notoriously gay and internationally famous playwright of *The Glass Menagerie, A Streetcar Named Desire and Cat on a Hot Tin Roof*, **Tennessee Williams** came to attend the burial of his father **Cornelius Coffin** "C.C." Williams in Old Gray Cemetery on Broadway.

Tennessee Williams and Marlon Brando

(By this point it should be obvious that if you're into graveyards, make time to take Henley Street (on the edge of the World's Fair Park) one mile north and visit the incredible **Old Gray Cemetery** on your left.)

Old Gray Cemetery

After returning to New York, Williams penned *Suddenly Last Summer*, his most painfully confessional play. In the play, an aunt wants her niece lobotomized at a mental institution named "Lyon's View."

This is interesting from a local standpoint in that Tennessee Williams' father, Cornelius Coffin was born in Knoxville, went to the University of Tennessee, and died here in Park Hotel. C.C. had chosen Knoxville's **Cherokee Country Club** (on **Lyon's View Road**) for his daughter's jazz-age debutante party in **1927**, where Tennessee William's sister **Rose** was spurned by a boy with whom she'd fallen in love.

After that public humiliation, Rose began exhibiting "erratic sexual behavior," was diagnosed as schizophrenic, and was institutionalized in her late 20s by her mother, at whose insistence Rose was lobotomized... just like Catherine in *Suddenly Last Summer*...

Tennessee Williams choice of the name "Lyon's View" for a fictional asylum resonates with Scruffy Citizens. Not only is Lyon's View the road leading to Cherokee Country Club, **East Tennessee Hospital for the Insane** was built on land previously owned by one **Captain William Lyon**, and opened in **1886** with 99 patients transferred from the **Tennessee Lunatic Asylum** in Nashville.

In **1977**, the hospital's name was changed to **Lakeshore Mental Institute**. In **1980**, it was decided to shift the mentally ill to the community and the percentage of mentally ill among the homeless jumped from 12% to 47%.

In **2012**, Lakeshore was closed entirely as part of another budget reduction and the area is now an attractive 185-acre public park.

Our point of course is that Tennessee Williams was yet another talented and troubled alcohol-and-drug-addicted writer with a strong Scruffy City connection.

When Williams died in **1983** his will left most of his estate in trust for his sister Rose. On her death, Tennessee Williams left the literary rights of his works to fund the creative writing program at **The University of the South** in **Sewanee, Tennessee**.

In one more interesting aside, in reference to the his first name, Williams often explained in interviews that he was honoring his direct ancestry to Knoxville's founder **James White**.

Lakeshore Mental Institute still stands in the midst of **Lakeshore Park**, located at **6410 South Northshore Drive**, although most of its buildings "for the insane" have decayed into ruin.

Throughout history, people with various mental disabilities were considered a threat to society, and as such they were disposed of. There was no treatment for them. Thus, **East Tennessee Hospital for the Insane** was essentially a prison for the mentally disabled.

The original Lakeshore Asylum building burned down in the **1920s**, but the ruins are still visible and some who have visited them say that they could hear screams of patients being beaten and abused by sadistic workers, as well as hear sounds of music boxes and clanking shackles. Visitors to the park sometimes have encounters with eerie shadow figures. Paranormal investigators like J. Adam Smith of Haunted Knoxville Ghost Tours believe that this is directly connected to the abundance of torture that occurred in the 165 years that East Tennessee Hospital for the Insane operated.

KEEP KNOXVILLE SCRUFFY

Support local food,
local music,
local culture,
local history
and local businesses!